Prince Edward Island

Prince Edward Island

Kumari Campbell

PARVA · SUB · INGENTI

Fitzhenry & Whiteside

Lerner website address: www.lernerbooks.com

Licensed to Fitzhenry & Whiteside for exclusive sale in Canada by arrangement with the Lerner Publishing Group

Fitzhenry & Whiteside
195 Allstate Parkway
Markham, ON L3R 4T8

Canadian Cataloguing in Publication

Campbell, Kumari, 1949–
    Prince Edward Island
(Hello Canada)
Includes index.
ISBN 1–55041–267–1
1. Prince Edward Island—Juvenile literature. I. Title. II. Series.
FC2611.2.C25 1998 j971.7 C98–930926–6
F1047.4.C25 1998
"A Micmac Legend" on page 21 is adapted from *Micmac Legends of Prince Edward Island* by John Joe Sark, © 1988 Ragweed Press, Charlottetown, Prince Edward Island. Used by permission.

Manufactured in the United States of America
2 3 4 5 6 7 – JR – 03 02 01 00 99 98

Cover photograph © John Sylvester. Background photo by R. Chen/SuperStock.

The glossary that starts on page 68 gives definitions of words shown in **bold type** in the text.

Senior Editor
Gretchen Bratvold
Editor
Colleen Sexton
Photo Researcher
Cindy Hartmon Nelson
Series Designer
Steve Foley
Designer
Julie Cisler

Our thanks to Boyde Beck of the Prince Edward Island Museum and Heritage Foundation and to Vince Warner, a curriculum specialist from the Prince Edward Island Department of Education, for their help in preparing this book.

 This book is printed on acid-free, recyclable paper.

Contents

Fun Facts

🍁 The coastal town of Souris—meaning "mouse" in French—got its name from large numbers of mice that used to overrun Prince Edward Island in the 1700s. Thousands of mice ate their way across the island's fields, destroying all the crops in their path.

🍁 In the late 1800s and early 1900s, some Prince Edward Islanders made a fortune raising silver foxes. The valuable furs were sold in Europe and made into fashionable coats and hats. With their earnings, the fox farmers built magnificent homes that became known as fox houses.

Hi! My name is Barkley. As you read *Prince Edward Island,* I will be helping you make sense of some of the maps and charts that appear in the book.

The chocolate milk and ice cream in your refrigerator may contain Irish moss from the sea around Prince Edward Island. The province is a big supplier of this red algae, which is used to thicken foods and other products, such as toothpaste and shoe polish.

Up until the late 1800s, the only way that Prince Edward Islanders could cross the frozen sea in winter was in small iceboats that made the dangerous trip to the Canadian mainland weekly. If the boat hit thick ice and couldn't break through, crew members strapped on leather harnesses and pulled the boats. Nowadays big ice-breaking ferries regularly transport people, cars, and trucks through frozen waters.

Guiding his horse out of the sea, a harvester hauls a load of Irish moss ashore.

In the early 1900s, fishermen caught so many lobsters in Prince Edward Island's waters that kids usually took lobster sandwiches to school. Bologna sandwiches were considered a special lunchtime treat! Nowadays lobsters are a delicacy.

7

The rows of a newly plowed field (facing page) *meet the sea. Lupines* (above) *thrive in Prince Edward Island's rich, red soil.*

The Garden of the Gulf

What is 140 miles (225 kilometers) long, completely surrounded by water, and rusty? Answer: Prince Edward Island. Also known by the initials P.E.I., this small island is covered with rich, rust-colored soil. Crops grow so well here that Prince Edward Island has earned the nickname the Garden of the Gulf.

Shaped like a crescent moon, Prince Edward Island fits snugly into the southern end of the salty Gulf of St. Lawrence, an arm of the North Atlantic Ocean. The waters of the Northumberland Strait—a narrow section of the gulf—wash against Prince Edward Island's southern shore.

An ice-breaking ferry pushes through the frozen Northumberland Strait, which separates P.E.I. from mainland Canada.

The strait separates P.E.I. from the mainland provinces of New Brunswick and Nova Scotia. Together these three provinces form the Maritime region of Canada. The Maritime provinces, along with the province of Newfoundland and Labrador to the northeast, make up Atlantic Canada.

Canada's smallest province, Prince Edward Island is about the size of the U.S. state of Delaware. The island would fit into the whole country of Canada about 1,000 times. Residents of Prince Edward Island are known as Islanders, and they call their province the Island.

P.E.I. hasn't always been an island. About 11,000 years ago, the island was connected to New Brunswick and Nova Scotia by a low plain. Then huge sheets of ice called **glaciers** moved over the

Colorful fields blanket much of Prince Edward Island.

plain. The glaciers were so thick and heavy that they pushed down the land. When the glaciers melted, they filled the ocean until water completely covered the plain, forming an island.

Nowadays most of P.E.I. is a gently rolling lowland, except for a small hilly section in the middle of the province. Here the highest point is only 466 feet (142 meters) above sea level.

From the air, Prince Edward Island looks like a giant patchwork quilt. Squares of small wooded areas, large patches of yellow grain, and huge fields of potatoes—Prince Edward Island's most important crop—cover the province. Some squares show rich, rust-colored soil. Large amounts of a mineral called iron oxide give the fertile soil its dark red color.

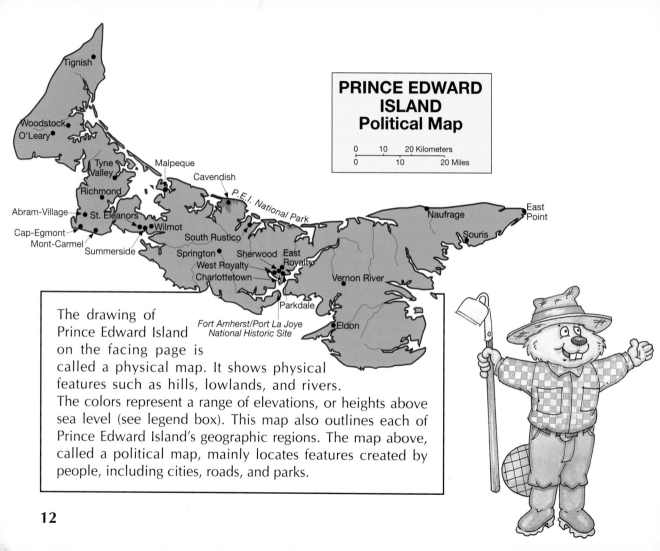

PRINCE EDWARD ISLAND Political Map

```
0        10      20 Kilometers
0            10        20 Miles
```

Tignish

Woodstock •
O'Leary •

Tyne Valley •

Malpeque

Cavendish

Richmond

P.E.I. National Park

Abram-Village

St. Eleanors

Naufrage

East Point

Cap-Egmont

Wilmot

Souris

Mont-Carmel

Summerside

South Rustico

Springton •

Sherwood

East Royalty

West Royalty

Charlottetown

Vernon River •

Parkdale

Fort Amherst/Port La Joye National Historic Site

Eldon

The drawing of Prince Edward Island on the facing page is called a physical map. It shows physical features such as hills, lowlands, and rivers. The colors represent a range of elevations, or heights above sea level (see legend box). This map also outlines each of Prince Edward Island's geographic regions. The map above, called a political map, mainly locates features created by people, including cities, roads, and parks.

12

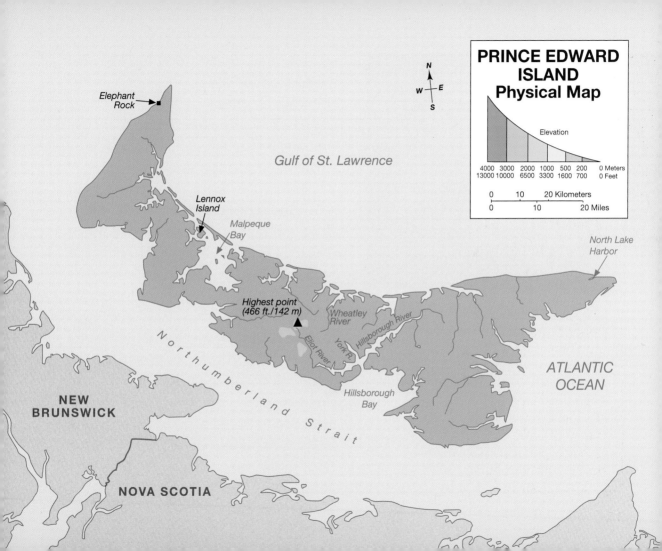

PRINCE EDWARD ISLAND Physical Map

Elevation

| 4000 | 3000 | 2000 | 1000 | 500 | 200 | 0 Meters |
| 13000 | 10000 | 6500 | 3300 | 1600 | 700 | 0 Feet |

0   10   20 Kilometers
0   10   20 Miles

N
W — E
S

Elephant Rock

Gulf of St. Lawrence

Lennox Island

Malpeque Bay

North Lake Harbor

Highest point (466 ft./142 m)

Wheatley River

Hillsborough River

Eliot River

York R.

Northumberland Strait

Hillsborough Bay

NEW BRUNSWICK

NOVA SCOTIA

ATLANTIC OCEAN

A fisherman casts his line into the Wheatley River in north-central P.E.I.

Among the patchwork squares, narrow tidal rivers wind across the Island. Seawater helps feed these waterways. The level of the ocean rises and falls twice each day with the **tides.** At high tide, seawater washes into the rivers.

At low tide, water flows back to sea. Away from the coast, the rivers shrink into small streams. Only a few tidal rivers in P.E.I. are large enough for canoeing or kayaking, but fishers snag trout in almost any stream.

Inlets of all sizes nick P.E.I.'s long coastline. The largest of these are Hillsborough Bay and Malpeque Bay. Small fishing villages line the coast, and some residents live on the few islands that dot the coastal waters. On shore, white-sand beaches and red-sand beaches stretch between rugged sandstone cliffs. Along the north shore, sand **dunes** shaped by the wind are held in place by the strong roots of marram grass. This beautiful coastline attracts thousands of swimmers, sailors, and sunbathers to the Island every summer.

Prince Edward Island's 688-mile (1,107-kilometer) coastline includes long beaches (left), *wind-sculpted sand dunes* (below), *and rugged cliffs* (right).

15

Lights reflect off the water in Charlottetown. The city is the cultural, educational, and economic center of Prince Edward Island.

Charlottetown is the Island's capital and largest city. P.E.I.'s chief port, Charlottetown is located on a wide harbor that opens to the Northumberland Strait. Three small rivers—the York, the Eliot, and the Hillsborough—meet to form this large harbor. About 4 out of 10 Islanders live in and around Charlottetown.

In Prince Edward Island, summers are cooler and winters are warmer than in other parts of Canada. In July the province's average temperature is 66° F (19° C), while readings dip to an average of 19° F (–7° C) in January. Rain and snow bring about 42 inches (107 centimeters) of **precipitation** to Prince Edward Island every year. This water soaks into the earth, where it feeds underground streams that provide the province with its water supply.

Sea ice surrounds the Island in winter and usually doesn't melt until the end of April. In the Gulf of St. Lawrence, sea ice is thin in some places and very thick in others. Large sections of ice called **floes** move with the ocean currents. Ice-breaking ferries push through the frozen sea to transport cars and trucks across the Northumberland Strait to the mainland. In spring sea ice sometimes gets in the way of lobster fishers, who start setting their traps in May.

Sea ice (above) *surrounds Prince Edward Island during the winter. In summer, warm weather brings clam diggers* (below) *to the seashore.*

While the ice can cause problems for people, it's a resting spot for many kinds of seals, especially harp seals, who give birth in the winter. Every year nature lovers venture onto the ice to see the baby harp seals. Throughout the year, a wide variety of other sea mammals—including whales and dolphins—make their homes in P.E.I.'s coastal waters. On land residents sometimes catch a glimpse of coyotes and red foxes. Beavers, muskrat, rabbits, raccoon, skunks, chipmunks, and squirrels also live on the Island.

Harbor seals (facing page) **bask on a rocky shore. Red foxes** (below) **live in the Island's wooded areas. A great blue heron** (right) **wades in the Island's coastal waters.**

Brown-eyed Susans and white asters brighten P.E.I.'s forests and fields.

More than 300 species of shorebirds visit Prince Edward Island every year. These birds—including piping plovers, cormorants, and black guillemots—travel between their winter homes in warmer climates far to the south and their summer homes in northern Canada. Other species—such as blue jays, ravens, sparrows, seagulls, hawks, and American bald eagles—are permanent residents of P.E.I.

Some of these birds make their homes in the Island's wooded areas. Heavy logging during the mid-1800s stripped the Island of its thick forests. But woodlands of maples, spruces, and white birches are thriving once again.

Wildflowers add color to P.E.I.'s landscape from May through October. In spring sweet-smelling mayflowers blossom. Millions of pink, purple, and white lupines cover fields and ditches in summer. The Island's most famous wildflower is the fragile lady's slipper, the province's official flower. This beautiful pink bloom signals that spring has once again arrived on Prince Edward Island.

A Micmac Legend

A long time ago, the Great Spirit who lived in the Happy Hunting Grounds created the universe and all life. After creating the universe, the Great Spirit sat down to rest. Then he created Glooscap and gave him special spiritual and physical powers. He called Glooscap to share the sacred pipe and said, "Glooscap, I am going to create a people in my image. I will call them Micmac."

The Great Spirit was pleased with his creation. He took out his sacred pipe and again called Glooscap. The Great Spirit noticed a large amount of dark red clay. "Glooscap, look at this large piece of clay, the same color as my Micmac people. I will shape this clay into a crescent form, and it will be the most beautiful of all places on Mother Earth. It will become the home of my Micmac people."

The Great Spirit fashioned an enchanting island and called it Minegoo. Minegoo was so beautiful that it made the Great Spirit extremely happy—so happy that he thought about placing Minegoo among the stars. After considering this for a short time, the Wise One decided that Minegoo should be placed in the middle of the singing waters, now known as the Gulf of St. Lawrence.

Prince Edward Island's first residents—Paleo-Indians—gathered berries in the island's thick forests and hunted sea mammals along the coast.

Settling by the Sea

About 11,000 years ago, what is now Prince Edward Island was connected to the mainland. Early peoples known as Paleo-Indians tracked caribou, arctic foxes, and other game through the region's thick forests. Along the coast, these hunters speared seals and walrus. When these animals became hard to find, Paleo-Indians left the Maritime region.

Maritime Archaic Indians moved into the area about 6,000 years ago. These coastal people journeyed into the forests in summer to gather berries and other plant foods. They fished and hunted large animals. From stones and bones, Maritime Archaic Indians carved tools and animal figures.

About 2,500 years ago, the Micmac Indians settled in the Maritime region. By this time, water separated what is now P.E.I. from the mainland. The Micmacs, who may have descended from the Maritime Archaic Indians, called their island Minegoo, meaning "the island." They gave it the nickname Abegweit, or "land cradled on the waves."

23

During the summer, many Micmac groups gathered on the northern coast of the island to fish, feast, and assign hunting regions. When fall drew near, the groups moved inland, where they built grass lodgings called **wigwams.** The Indians covered these shelters with furs for the cold winter. When the Micmacs hunted, they often traveled the island's rivers in birchbark canoes. Hunters sometimes had to portage, or carry, their canoes from river to river.

Micmac elders taught children by telling stories about the past and about nature. They also talked about the Great Spirit, who, to the Micmacs, was the creator of all things. At an early age, children learned to fish, hunt, and gather berries and herbs.

The Micmacs' way of life began to change in the 1500s, when Europeans first set foot on the island's shores. Jacques Cartier, who was exploring the region for France, landed on what is now Prince Edward Island in 1534. Cartier claimed all the land that he saw for France. Over time the French came to call this region L'Acadie, or Acadia. Acadia included almost all of what is now southeastern Canada plus part of the present-day U.S. state of Maine. The French named the island, which was part of Acadia, Ile-Saint-Jean.

During the next 100 years, people from Spain, Portugal, France, and England also came to Acadia to fish for cod. Some said the island's coastal waters were so thick with fish that they slowed the boats. Fishing crews loaded their vessels with cod and other fish to sell in Europe.

The Micmac Indians traveled the Maritime region's waterways in birchbark canoes and set up camps on shore.

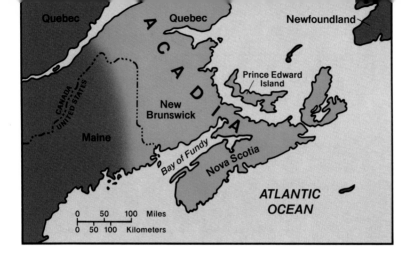

Acadia (left) *stretched from what is now southeastern Canada to the present-day U.S. state of Maine. By the 1720s, the Acadians had built sturdy farmhouses* (facing page) *in small settlements.*

Before returning home, the fishermen dried the fish on wooden racks in the sun. While working at their shoreline camps, the Europeans met Micmacs. The fishers traded metal tools, guns, and clothing with the Native people in exchange for furs, which were very valuable in Europe.

In the early 1600s, French officials wanted to gain control of fishing waters and the fur trade in Acadia. France soon established a **colony,** or settlement, at Port Royal in what is now Nova Scotia. The first colonists were followed by French farmers. Together the French settlers came to be called Acadians.

Although the French set up the first colony in Acadia, the British also claimed fishing and fur-trading rights in the region. The two countries battled over this valuable territory throughout the 1600s. In 1713 France and Britain signed the Treaty of Utrecht, which gave what are now Newfoundland, New Brunswick, and mainland Nova Scotia to Britain. France kept Ile-Saint-Jean and what are now Québec and Cape Breton Island (now part of Nova Scotia).

Until this time, both France and Britain had ignored Ile-Saint-Jean, and neither country had built a settlement on the island. Some Acadians left Nova Scotia to farm Ile-Saint-Jean's fertile red soil. And in 1720, a group of colonists from France joined the Acadians. Near what is now Charlottetown, the colonists built Port La Joye and made it their capital. During the next 20 years, French settlements also sprang up along the northern and eastern shores of the island.

The newcomers cleared forests for farmland, built churches, and made trails to link their new communities. But life was very difficult for the settlers. Field mice and forest fires often destroyed the crops, leaving the colonists without enough food.

The Micmacs, who had traditionally stalked their prey with bows and arrows, learned to hunt with guns. Canoes helped the Indians travel quickly through their hunting grounds.

28

The Micmacs helped the Acadians survive. The Indians showed the newcomers how to hunt and where to fish. They also taught the settlers how to canoe the island's rivers and how to cross deep snow in snowshoes. And when the Acadians were sick, the Native people took care of them.

The Micmacs also came to depend on the Acadians, who traded manufactured supplies, such as tools and wool blankets, for valuable furs. This trade helped the two groups live in peace. But contact with the Acadians also brought hardship to some Micmacs. Native people died from diseases carried by the Europeans.

While the Native population of Ile-Saint-Jean dwindled, the number of colonists grew. Meanwhile, in Nova Scotia, tensions were increasing between the British and the Acadians. About 2,000 Acadians escaped British soldiers and fled to Ile-Saint-Jean. This sudden increase in people made food and shelter scarce on the island. Living conditions worsened. Most Acadians became dependent on the faraway French government to send food and supplies.

In 1756 the French and the British again began battling for North America. This conflict was part of the Seven Years' War, which was also being fought in Europe. Within two years, the British had captured the French Fortress of Louisbourg on Cape Breton Island. This stronghold had protected all of France's territories in the Maritime region. With the fall of the fortress, France lost control of its territories in what is now eastern Canada.

The British ordered all Acadians to leave Ile-Saint-Jean. British soldiers loaded the settlers onto ships bound for France. In all, the British forced about 3,000 Acadians from the island. Only 30 Acadian families, who had managed to hide from British soldiers, remained behind. When the Seven Years' War ended in 1763, Britain translated the name of the island into English, calling it Saint John's Island.

The next year, the British king assigned Captain Samuel Holland to measure the size and shape of Saint John's Island. Holland divided the island into 67 townships, which were given to wealthy subjects of the king. The new owners—called landlords—had to pay rent to the British government each year. The landlords were also required to bring settlers to the island.

Of the 3,000 Acadians forced from their homes (left), ***700 drowned when their ships sank in the Atlantic Ocean. British settlers later moved to the island and founded Charlottetown*** (facing page).

The first British settlers began arriving on Saint John's Island in 1768. Charlottetown—which had been built across the harbor from Port La Joye—became the capital. The British government appointed Captain Walter Patterson as governor of the island. In 1773 residents elected the colony's first Assembly to run local affairs. The Assembly brought residents' concerns to the governor and his council, an appointed group of advisers.

In the late 1700s, at the request of the Assembly, Patterson asked the British king to change the name of Saint John's Island because many other places in the region had the same name. So in 1799, the colony was renamed Prince Edward Island in honor of the king's son.

By the early 1800s, tenant farmers had cleared much of P.E.I.'s land, and logging and shipbuilding industries were booming.

The Cradle of Confederation

Walter Patterson and other governors struggled to develop Prince Edward Island during the early 1800s. Many of the British landlords hadn't moved to Prince Edward Island to oversee their land, and some weren't even paying their rent. Without this money, Prince Edward Island's government couldn't build roads and towns. Settlers had to work hard to create a colony by themselves.

By 1805 P.E.I.'s population had swelled to 7,000 people, most of whom came from Scotland and Ireland. These **immigrants** became tenant farmers, who rented large plots from landlords. The tenants farmed for many years before they could grow enough crops to make extra money. In the meantime, many tenants fell behind on the rent and worried that the landlords would take away their farms.

As farmers cleared the land, other settlers hauled the trees to small shipyards on the coast. Here workers sawed the timber into planks to make large, oceangoing vessels. Many skilled laborers—including carpenters, sailmakers, and blacksmiths—found work building ships. By the 1830s, more than 100 shipyards lined Prince Edward Island's coast.

Around this time, tension was building between tenant farmers and landlords. Angered that they didn't have the right to buy land, some farmers refused to pay their rent. Sometimes they attacked the landlords. In time some landlords agreed to sell their townships. But instead of selling to farmers, the land was quickly snatched up by wealthy Islanders, who, in turn, also demanded rent.

In 1842 a wealthy merchant and landowner named George Coles was elected to P.E.I.'s Assembly. Coles, who grew up on a tenant farm, believed that the best way to solve the problems between landlords and tenants—which had become known as the Land Question—was to change the way that the Island was governed.

In 1851 Britain gave Prince Edward Island **responsible government.** This meant that the governor's council would be made up of Assembly members elected by the public. Both the Council and the Assembly were then responsible, or answerable, to the Island's residents rather than to the British king.

With responsible government, Islanders could now change the land laws. In 1853 the Assembly passed

In 1864 officials met in Charlottetown to talk about forming the Dominion of Canada.

the Land Purchase Act. This new law allowed P.E.I.'s government to buy land from the landlords and sell it to tenant farmers. Over the next 20 years, the tenants bought about one-third of the Island.

During the mid-1800s, the Maritime colonies—along with other British colonies to the west—were talking about uniting as one country. In 1864 officials met in Charlottetown to discuss this idea. After three years of debate, Nova Scotia, New Brunswick, Ontario, and Québec formed a new country called the Dominion of Canada. The official union—or **Confederation**—of these colonies took place on July 1, 1867.

Shipbuilders used logs felled from P.E.I.'s forests to construct huge, oceangoing vessels.

For its role in creating a new country, P.E.I. was nicknamed the Cradle of Confederation. But residents of Prince Edward Island decided not to join Canada. Being physically cut off from the mainland gave Islanders a sense of independence. They felt proud of their unique island way of life and were satisfied with their colonial government.

In addition, after many years of hard work, Islanders had begun to prosper. The lumber and shipbuilding industries were booming, and farmers and fishers were earning big profits. Islanders believed that if they joined Canada, they would have to share this wealth. And with a population much smaller than the other provinces, the Island would not have much of a voice in the new Canadian government.

In the 1870s, however, P.E.I.'s good fortune ran out when the colony's government decided to build a railroad. Every community and landowner wanted the Prince Edward Island Railway to pass by their property. To make a railroad with so many stations, the government had to borrow money. Soon the Island had a huge debt.

Then the Canadian government made P.E.I. an offer it couldn't refuse. If Prince Edward Island entered the Confederation, the Dominion would pay the Island's debt, operate the railroad, and make sure that steamships and telegraphs linked the Island to the mainland. The Canadian government would also give P.E.I. six seats in the Canadian parliament. On July 1, 1873, Prince Edward Island became the seventh Canadian province.

Many Islanders found jobs building the Prince Edward Island Railway.

Potato farming grew into a big business on Prince Edward Island during the 1900s.

Confederation didn't solve all of the Island's problems, however. When steel steamships began replacing wooden sailing vessels in the late 1870s, P.E.I.'s shipbuilding industry collapsed. Thousands of Islanders moved to the eastern United States, where shipbuilding was still booming.

Those who stayed behind continued to farm or fish for a living. Farmers grew potatoes and grains, while fishers caught cod, herring, and mackerel. Lobster fishing became a big business after new canning methods were developed in the late 1800s.

P.E.I.'s canneries bustled during World War II (1939–1945), when huge quantities of canned fish were sent overseas to feed troops from Canada and other countries. Local farmers also grew more crops to feed soldiers. Military bases in P.E.I. trained soldiers, who helped the province's economy by buying goods from local merchants.

When the war ended, many of these activities came to a halt, and Islanders had trouble finding work. Many residents left P.E.I. to look for jobs in the cities of central and western Canada. In 1969 P.E.I.'s government came up with a plan to encourage people to stay on the Island. The government offered construction jobs building new schools, hospitals, and roads—projects that would help improve life for Islanders.

Throughout the 1900s, Islanders had discussed whether P.E.I. should be connected to the mainland. In 1993 the government decided to build a bridge across the Northumberland Strait. The bridge—or fixed link, as Islanders call it—would make travel to and from the Island easier. Local business leaders argue that if trucks and cars—which now have to wait for ferries—can get to the Island faster, more companies will move to P.E.I. These businesses would bring new jobs and more money to the province. But many residents worry that the fixed link will rob them of their unique island way of life.

The fixed link is a troublesome issue for many Islanders. They value their quiet lifestyle but also want to attract new businesses to the province. As in the past, residents are faced with a difficult decision—to improve their economy, they might have to give up some of their independence.

From the Soil and the Sea

With lots of rich farmland, it's no wonder that P.E.I. has nicknames such as the Garden of the Gulf, the Million Acre Farm, and Spud Island. About 2,800 farms spread across Prince Edward Island's rolling red landscape. And crops take up half of the Island's land area.

Lobster traps line the docks (above) *at North Lake Harbor near P.E.I.'s northeastern tip. Farmers harvest potatoes* (facing page left) *grown in the Island's fertile fields* (facing page right).

A dairy farmer in Vernon River runs his farm with the help of a computer.

Farmers make up 7 percent of P.E.I.'s workforce, and agriculture earns more money than any other industry in the province. The Island's soil and climate are best suited for growing potatoes, the province's most important crop. Three-fourths of the potatoes grown on P.E.I. are seed potatoes, which are sold around the world to other farmers who plant them in their fields to grow more potatoes. Table potatoes, which are sold fresh in markets, make up the rest of the crop.

Island farmers also raise strawberries, raspberries, blueberries, peas, cabbages, carrots, and beans. And they grow enough oats, barley, and wheat to feed their livestock, including hogs, chickens, and beef cattle. Milk from the province's dairy cows is processed into butter, cheese, and yogurt.

Some farms on the Island have become big businesses. For example, farmers use computer systems and advanced machinery to plan for, plant, and harvest crops. But as the Island's farms have grown, farmers have been using more fertilizers and pesticides on their fields. These chemicals, which help produce more crops and drive away unwanted insects, can harm the environment.

Animals that eat plants sprayed with certain chemicals can die. Fertilizers and pesticides can pollute rivers and kill fish. Many scientists believe the chemicals even cause diseases in people. To reduce the amount of chemicals used on the Island, some small farms use organic, or natural, fertilizers such as manure (animal waste). But because organic fertilizers take more time to spread on crops, people who own large farms still rely on chemicals.

The fishery, or fishing industry, is another big business in the province, employing about 5 percent of the workforce. Fishers on P.E.I. mainly catch lobsters. The Island is also fa-mous for its Malpeque oysters, which are harvested from Malpeque Bay in western P.E.I. Other fish caught in the Island's waters include hake, flounder, herring, and mackerel.

A fisher displays a string of mussels.

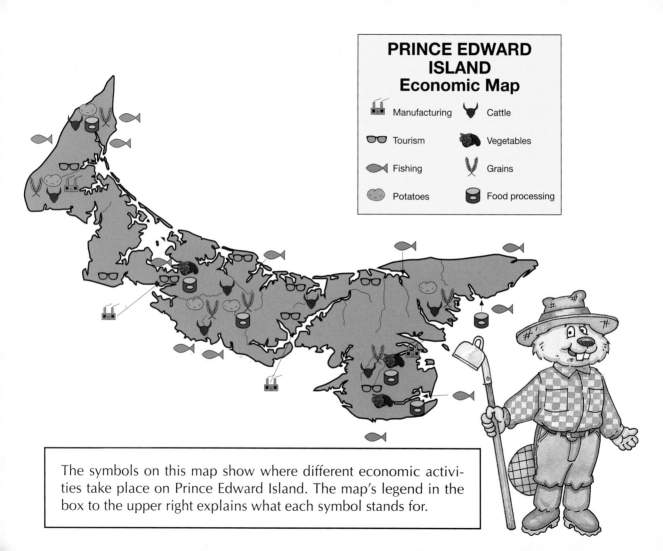

**PRINCE EDWARD ISLAND
Economic Map**

🏭	Manufacturing	🐂	Cattle
👓	Tourism	🥦	Vegetables
🐟	Fishing	🌾	Grains
🥔	Potatoes	🥫	Food processing

The symbols on this map show where different economic activities take place on Prince Edward Island. The map's legend in the box to the upper right explains what each symbol stands for.

Loads of Lobsters

David's workday begins long before most people even see the light of day. In fact when David wakes up at 4 A.M., he doesn't see the light of day either! David is a lobster fisher on Prince Edward Island.

At 5 A.M., David meets his helper Mike at Naufrage Harbor along the northeastern coast of P.E.I. David starts his boat, and the fishers head for the lobster buyer's station on the wharf, where David buys bait for the day—usually herring or mackerel. Then they are ready to head out to sea and to David's 300 traps, or pots.

David's pots are divided into groups of eight, each of which is attached to a strong cord called a trawl line. A buoy at the end of the line helps David and Mike find the traps. The locations of all of the lines are programmed into a computerized navigation device. So David and Mike just enter the locations on the computer, which then gives them directions to the pots. With the help of a compass, David and Mike soon reach the first trawl line.

Mike uses a machine called a hydraulic hauler to lift the pots out of the water. The two fishers then remove the lobsters from the traps and measure them. If they are smaller than the minimum size allowed by fishery officials, they are too young to be caught. So David and Mike throw these lobsters back. The rest of the lobsters go into a holding tank. The two fishers then rebait the traps and put them back in the water.

When all 300 pots have been emptied and rebaited, David guides his boat back to shore. The last stop is at the buyer's station, where David sells his catch. At 1:20 P.M., David and Mike drop anchor back in Naufrage Harbor.

The number of lobsters and other kinds of fish in the North Atlantic Ocean has been dropping in recent years. So the Canadian government has set quotas, or limits, on how many fish can be caught. With less fishing allowed, lobsters and other species will have a chance to multiply. This increase will help keep the Island's fishery strong.

P.E.I.'s fish and farm goods are processed and packaged at the Island's factories. Some manufacturers specialize in preparing fish fillets. Others make potatoes into potato chips or frozen french fries. Still others produce clothing, fertilizers, or medical instruments. About 8 percent of the province's workers have manufacturing jobs.

Most Islanders—73 percent—work in the service industry. Service workers

Food-processing workers pack lobsters at a canning plant in Tignish.

help other people and businesses. Salespeople, politicians, accountants, lawyers, dry cleaners, dentists, and truck drivers all hold service jobs. The biggest service industry on Prince Edward Island is tourism. People who work in this industry guide tours, run hotels, or prepare and serve food in restaurants.

A server shows off the main course of a lobster supper, a traditional meal offered in many Island communities.

Tourists flock to P.E.I. to enjoy sandy beaches, quiet surroundings, and the friendly people of this small island. Prince Edward Island is also famous as the setting for the book *Anne of Green Gables* by Lucy Maud Montgomery. Thousands of people come to the Island each year to visit the Green Gables House in Cavendish and other places described in the book. Every year at the Charlottetown Festival, tickets sell out for performances of a musical version of the book.

Some visitors to Prince Edward Island are interested in seeing the birds and animals that live on the Island. Islanders hope that their newest idea—called the Rails-to-Trails project—will bring more nature-loving tourists to P.E.I. Project workers are turning the old Prince Edward Island Railway into

A girl poses as Anne, the main character in the book Anne of Green Gables. *The places described in this famous story, which is set on the Island, draw thousands of tourists to P.E.I. every year.*

a trail that stretches from one end of the Island to the other. Islanders and visitors will be able to hike or bike along the rail line, which will be called the Confederation Trail. This new attraction gives residents the opportunity to show off their beautiful island from tip to tip.

The Island Way of Life

If you page through a P.E.I. telephone directory, you'll probably notice right away how thick the "M" section is. Family names beginning with "Mac" fill up more than half the phone book! This is because the majority of Islanders have ancestors from Scotland, and "Mac" is a common beginning for Scottish last names.

Music is an important part of the Scottish heritage. At celebrations called Ceilidhs, fiddlers and bagpipers play while dancers step in time to the music. Ceilidh performers often dress in kilts—skirts with plaid patterns called **tartans.** Singers perform some songs in Gaelic, the traditional language of the Highland Scots.

In all, about 80 percent of Prince Edward Island's residents have European backgrounds. Many Islanders claim ancestors from Ireland, England, and France. Other Islanders are of

Wearing tartan kilts and scarves, Scottish dancers (left) *perform in front of Province House, the headquarters of P.E.I.'s government. At the Multicultural Festival in Charlottetown, Islanders display goods* (facing page left) *and perform dances* (facing page right) *from other countries.*

Dutch, Polish, German, or Ukrainian heritage. In the late 1800s, a small group of settlers came to P.E.I. from Lebanon, a country in the Middle East.

Many of their descendants still live on the Island. Newcomers from Japan, China, India, Hungary, and Mexico have also settled on the Island.

Dressed in traditional costumes, Acadians in Abram-Village celebrate their heritage.

Acadians, who make up about 12 percent of the population, live mainly in western P.E.I. Many Acadians speak French in their homes and businesses, and some Acadian children attend French-language schools.

Acadian craftspeople, who make clothing, quilts, and pottery just as their ancestors did, sell their wares in small shops on the Island. At the annual National Acadian Festival in Mont-Carmel, Acadians share their traditional songs, dances, and foods with other Islanders.

Micmacs make up less than 1 percent of P.E.I.'s population. Most Island

Micmacs live on three **reserves,** the largest of which is the Lennox Island Micmac Reserve. Here the Micmacs make their own laws and run their own government. English is the most common language among the Micmacs, but some Native people still speak the Micmac language.

No matter which ethnic group residents belong to, they identify themselves first as Islanders. With a population of only 134,557, it sometimes seems as if everyone in the province knows one another. Without bustling cities and big businesses, the province is largely free of pollution and has very little crime. Islanders enjoy a slow-paced, quiet way of life.

A Micmac artist on Lennox Island weaves a basket.

Harness racing is a popular sport on Prince Edward Island.

Residents turn out in droves to celebrate Island life. Nearly every community invites Islanders and visitors alike to local festivals. The P.E.I. Potato Blossom Festival in O'Leary, for example, honors the province's most important crop. The Island's famous oysters are featured at the P.E.I. Oyster Festival in Tyne Valley.

In winter, hardy Islanders head to the Charlottetown Winter Carnival for skiing and skating competitions. And throughout the summer, traditional lobster suppers draw big crowds. Offered in small communities all across the Island, these meals feature boiled lobsters and a tasty variety of vegetables, salads, and desserts.

Art and history buffs find plenty to see at the Confederation Centre of the Arts in Charlottetown, which houses a theater, two art galleries, and a library. At the Mill River Fun Park in Woodstock, kids of all ages enjoy water slides, a miniature golf course, and a zoo, where kids can play with animals.

No matter what the season, Islanders like to spend time outdoors. Swimmers, boaters, and surfers flock to the beaches all summer long. The white shores and tall sand dunes of Prince Edward Island National Park in Cavendish draw the biggest crowds. But because long stretches of sand surround the Island, there's plenty of

Wind and water shaped part of P.E.I.'s northwestern coast into Elephant Rock, a favorite spot for Islanders.

beach for everyone. Islanders also like to golf P.E.I.'s many courses and play baseball and soccer. Hiking, biking, and horseback riding on the Island's nature trails are popular warm-weather pastimes, too.

In winter Islanders head to the nearest patch of ice for a game of hockey.

Like other Canadians, Islanders are big hockey fans. Most kids learn to ice-skate almost as soon as they can walk. In winter, hockey players pass the puck in skating arenas and on frozen ponds. Curling, another ice sport, also attracts big crowds. In this game, teams slide stones down an icy lane and see who can hit or come closest to a target stone at the far end. To view the winter scenery, many Islanders glide along trails on cross-country skis.

With its beautiful beaches, rolling hills, rich cultural heritage, and quiet way of life, Canada's smallest province has a lot to offer. And these are just a few of the many reasons that both Islanders and visitors alike say P.E.I. is one of the world's greatest islands.

A windsurfer rides the waves off P.E.I.'s coast.

Famous Islanders

Milton Acorn (1923–1986), born in Charlottetown, was a poet who wrote about Island life and about the working men and women of Canada. In 1970 leading Canadian writers named him the "People's Poet of Canada." Acorn's collections include *I've Tasted My Blood* and *The Island Means Minago,* for which he won the Governor General's Award in 1976.

Angele Arsenault (born 1943) is a collector and singer of Acadian folk songs. In 1979 she won an ADISO Gala Award for her best-selling album *Libre.* Arsenault was born in Abrams, Prince Edward Island.

3 **Georges Arsenault** (born 1952), a former professor of Acadian studies at the University of Prince Edward Island, is a writer and broadcaster. His book *The Island Acadians* won the 1988 Prix France-Acadie Award. Arsenault was born in Abram-Village, P.E.I.

4 **George-Antoine Belcourt** (1803–1874) was a Roman Catholic missionary who worked on Prince Edward Island. Belcourt founded the Farmers' Bank of South Rustico, which was the forerunner of modern credit unions.

5 **Francis W. P. Bolger** (born 1925), from Stanley Ridge, P.E.I., wrote about Prince Edward Island and about writer Lucy Maud Montgomery. Bolger has also taught history at Saint Dunstan's University on P.E.I. and at the University of Prince Edward Island.

Carl F. Burke (1913–1976), born in Charlottetown, founded Maritime Central Airways, the largest independent cargo airline in Canada. Burke started the venture after serving as a pilot during World War II.

7 Catherine Callbeck (born 1939) is a politician and businesswoman from Central Bedeque, P.E.I. After working in her family's businesses—a furniture store and a chain of hardware outlets—Callbeck served four years in parliament. In 1993 she became Prince Edward Island's premier—the first elected woman premier in Canada.

Stompin' Tom Connors (born 1936), who grew up in Skinner's Pond, P.E.I., has written more than 500 songs, mostly about working people and small-town life. His 1990 album *A Proud Canadian* has sold more than 100,000 copies.

9 J. Regis Duffy (born 1932) founded Diagnostic Chemicals, Ltd., the first chemical plant on Prince Edward Island. He started the company after working as a chemistry professor at Saint Dunstan's University. Duffy was born in Kinkora, P.E.I.

10 Joseph Ghiz (born 1945), from Charlottetown, is a lawyer and politician. In 1981 he became the leader of P.E.I.'s liberal party. From 1986 to 1992, he served as the province's premier. Ghiz, who is of Lebanese descent, became the first person of a non-British background to hold this post in P.E.I.

11 George Godfrey (1852–1901), born in Charlottetown, was a prize-winning boxer. He was an American Black Heavyweight Champion and one of the best heavyweight fighters of the 1880s. During his career, Godfrey fought more than 100 boxing matches.

12 **Robert Harris** (1849–1919), who moved to P.E.I. from Wales when he was seven years old, was an artist known for his portraits of famous people. His best-known painting is *The Fathers of Confederation.* In 1893 Harris was elected president of the Royal Canadian Academy.

13 **Elsie Inman** (1890–1986) appeared before the legislature in 1920 to fight for the right of women to vote. She was later appointed a senator and organized the Liberal Women of Prince Edward Island. Inman was born in West River, P.E.I.

14 **David (Eli) MacEachern** (born 1967) was a 1994 World Cup Champion in the two-man bobsledding event. A brakeman for the Canadian national bobsledding team, he has also competed in the Olympic Games. MacEachern is from Charlottetown.

15 **Angus MacEachern** (1759–1835) came to live on Prince Edward Island in 1790 as a Catholic missionary from Scotland. In 1829 he was named the first bishop of a region that included P.E.I., New Brunswick, and the nearby Magdalen Islands. MacEachern also founded Saint Andrew's College on P.E.I.

16 **Andrew MacPhail** (1864–1938), born in Orwell, P.E.I., was a physician, teacher, and author. For 30 years, he taught courses in the history of medicine at McGill University in Montreal, Québec. MacPhail wrote more than ten books, including *The Master's Wife,* a novel about life on the Island in the 1800s.

17 **Lucy Maud Montgomery** (1874–1942) was an author who grew up in Cavendish, P.E.I. She used the Island as a setting for many of her books, the most famous of which is *Anne of Green Gables*. Montgomery published 23 books and more than 900 poems during her lifetime.

Joe O'Brien (1917–1984), born in Alberton, P.E.I., was a driver and trainer of harness horses. Considered one of the world's best harness racers, O'Brien drove the mile in under two minutes more times than any other driver. O'Brien also set the world's record for pacing.

19 **Michael Thomas** (1883–1954) was one of the top long-distance runners in eastern Canada. A member of the Abegweit Amateur Athletic Club, he won the Halifax Herald 10-mile road race three times and ran in the Boston Marathon. Thomas, who was born on Lennox Island, P.E.I., was a member of the Lennox Island Micmac Band.

20 **Mona Wilson** (1894–1981) was a nurse who helped teach Islanders about nutrition and health care. Considered a pioneer in public health, Wilson helped found the Junior Red Cross clubs, which taught P.E.I. residents about healthy living.

Fast Facts

Provincial Symbols

Motto: *Parva Sub Ingenti* (The small under the protection of the great)
Nicknames: The Cradle of Confederation, The Garden of the Gulf, The Million Acre Farm, Spud Island
Song: "The Island Hymn"
Flower: lady's slipper
Tree: northern red oak
Bird: blue jay
Tartan: reddish brown for the redness of the soil, green for the grass and the trees, white for the caps on the waves, and yellow for the sun

Provincial Highlights

Landmarks: Green Gables House in Cavendish, Elmira Railway Museum near Souris, Fort Amherst/Port La Joye National Historic Site, Basin Head Fisheries Museum near East Point, Prince Edward Island National Park in Cavendish, Mill River Fun Park in Woodstock, Elephant Rock in Norway, Potato Museum in O'Leary, the Bottle Houses in Cap-Egmont

Annual events: Charlottetown Winter Carnival in Charlottetown (Feb.), East Prince Music Festival in Summerside (May), Charlottetown Festival in Charlottetown (June), "Amazing Grace" Scottish Concert in Richmond (June), P.E.I. Potato Blossom Festival in O'Leary (July), Irish Moss Festival in Tignish (July), P.E.I. Oyster Festival in Tyne Valley (Aug.), Harvest Home Festival in Queens County (Oct.)

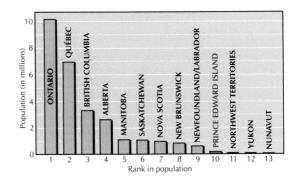

Population: 134,557
Rank in population, nationwide: 10th
Population distribution: 40 percent urban; 60 percent rural
Population density: 59.3 people per sq mi (23 per sq km)
Capital: Charlottetown (15,396*)
Major communities (and populations*): Summerside (7,474), Sherwood (6,006), Saint Eleanors (3,514), West Royalty (3,142), Parkdale (2,198), Wilmot (2,176), East Royalty (2,052)
Major ethnic groups*: British , 44 percent; multiple backgrounds, 44 percent; French, 9 percent; Dutch, 1 percent; German, 1 percent; Native peoples, Polish, Scandinavian, Ukrainian, 1 percent total

Endangered Species

Bird: piping plover

Geographic Highlights

Area (land/water): 2,185 sq mi (5,660 sq km)
Rank in area, nationwide: 13th
Highest point: Springton (466 ft/142 m)
Rivers: Hillsborough, York, Eliot

Economy

Percentage of Workers Per Job Sector

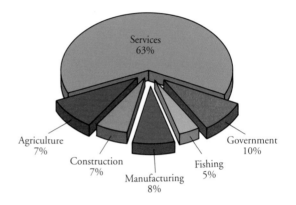

Services 63%
Agriculture 7%
Construction 7%
Manufacturing 8%
Fishing 5%
Government 10%

Natural resources: rich soil, fish, Irish moss, sand and gravel, natural gas, uranium, gold
Agricultural products: potatoes, barley, tobacco, vegetables, hay, beef and dairy cattle, hogs
Manufactured goods: potato chips, french fries, canned lobster, clothes, fertilizers, medical instruments

Energy

Electric power: P.E.I. imports 90 percent of its electricity from New Brunswick through a cable under the Northumberland Strait. This power comes from many sources, including nuclear energy, oil, and coal.

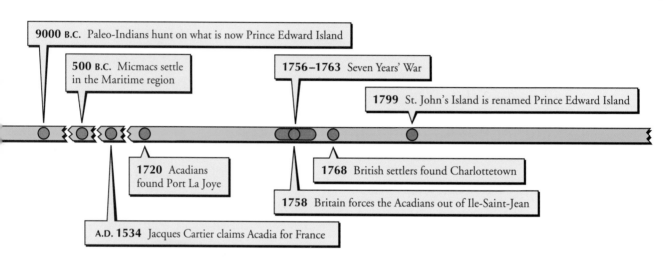

9000 B.C. Paleo-Indians hunt on what is now Prince Edward Island

500 B.C. Micmacs settle in the Maritime region

1756–1763 Seven Years' War

1799 St. John's Island is renamed Prince Edward Island

1720 Acadians found Port La Joye

1768 British settlers found Charlottetown

1758 Britain forces the Acadians out of Ile-Saint-Jean

A.D. 1534 Jacques Cartier claims Acadia for France

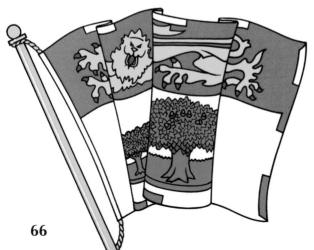

Federal Government

Capital: Ottawa

Head of state: British Crown, represented by the governor general

Head of government: prime minister

Cabinet: ministers appointed by the prime minister

Parliament: Senate—104 members appointed by the governor general; House of Commons—295 members elected by the people

Prince Edward Island representation in parliament: 4 senators; 4 house members

Voting age: 18

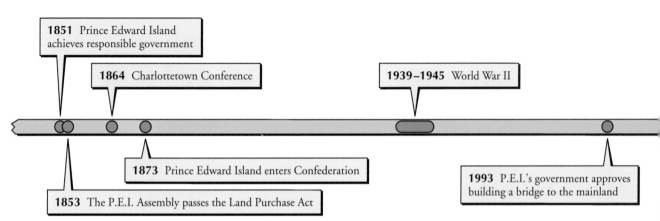

1851 Prince Edward Island achieves responsible government

1864 Charlottetown Conference

1939–1945 World War II

1873 Prince Edward Island enters Confederation

1853 The P.E.I. Assembly passes the Land Purchase Act

1993 P.E.I.'s government approves building a bridge to the mainland

Provincial Government

Capital: Charlottetown
Crown representative: lieutenant governor
Head of government: premier
Cabinet: ministers appointed by the premier
Legislative Assembly: 32 members elected to terms that can last up to five years
Voting age: 18
Major political parties: Liberal, New Democratic, Progressive Conservative

Government Services

To help pay the people who work for Prince Edward Island's government, Islanders pay taxes on money they earn and on many of the items they buy. The services run by the provincial government help assure Islanders of a high quality of life. Government funds pay for medical care, for education, for road building and repairs, and for other facilities such as libraries and parks. In addition, the government has funds to help people who are disabled, elderly, or poor.

Glossary

colony   A territory ruled by a country some distance away.

Confederation   The union of four British colonies under the British North America Act in 1867. Confederation formed the Dominion of Canada and set up two levels of government—national and provincial. Other provinces later joined the original four.

dune   A hill or ridge of sand piled up by the wind.

floe   Large sheets of ice that float on the surface of a body of water.

glacier   A large body of ice and snow that moves slowly over land.

immigrant   A person who moves into a foreign country and settles there.

precipitation   Rain, snow, and other forms of moisture that fall to earth.

reserve   Public land set aside by the government to be used by Native peoples.

responsible government   A form of government that made the governor responsible (answerable) to an assembly elected by the people.

tartan   A plaid pattern with stripes of different widths and colors originally worn by the Scots in Scotland. Each clan, or group of families, has its own pattern.

tide   The alternate rising and falling of the level of the ocean. Tides are caused by the position of the moon and the sun in relation to the earth.

wigwam   A kind of tent used by some Indian groups. The tent is shaped in a dome or cone and covered with bark, grasswoven mats, leaves, or other natural material.

Pronunciation Guide

Acadia (uh-KAY-dee-uh)

Cartier, Jacques
(kahr-TYAY, ZHAHK)

Ceilidh (KAY-lee)

Ile-Saint-Jean (eel-saynt-ZHAWN)

Malpeque (MAHL-pehk)

Minegoo (MIHN-ee-goh)

Port La Joye (PORT lah ZHWAH)

Souris (SOO-ree)

Index

About the Author

A freelance writer and editor, Kumari Campbell also owns her own marketing and public relations business. Originally from Sri Lanka, she moved to Canada when she was a teenager. Campbell lives with her husband and three children in Souris, Prince Edward Island.

Acknowledgments

Mapping Specialists Ltd., pp. 1, 12, 13, 44; © John Sylvester, pp. 2, 9, 10, 14, 15 (all), 16, 17 (both), 19 (both), 22, 40, 41 (both), 42, 43, 46-47, 48, 50, 51, 52, 53 (both), 55, 56, 59, 69, 71; Artwork by Terry Boles, pp. 6, 12, 44, 65; Jerry Hennen, pp. 7, 57; Voscar, The Maine Photographer, pp. 8, 18, 20, 45, 68; Canadian Tourism Commission, pp. 11, 54; © Lydia Parker, p. 21; Nova Scotia Museum, Halifax, pp. 25, 27; National Archives of Canada, pp. 31 (C277), 32 (C30280), 35 (C733), 38 (PA43964); Laura Westlund, p. 26; National Gallery of Canada, Ottawa, p. 28; Lewis Parker, Artist/Commissioned by Canadian Heritage (Parks Canada), Atlantic Region, p. 30; Prince Edward Island Public Archives and Records Office, pp. 36 (2301/237), 37 (2767/35), 60 (top left—2330/H-142), 61 (middle right—4249/1), 62 (top—3119/1), 62 (middle right—2320/67-9), 62 (middle left—2320/70-3), 62 (bottom right—2320/2-12), 63 (top—2320/38-1), 63 (bottom left—2320/29-12), 63 (bottom right—2320/98-10); Norma Watts, p. 49; © David C. Schultz, pp. 58, 70; Bob Maillet Photography, p. 60 (top right); Father Francis W.P. Bolger, p. 60 (bottom right); Diagnostic Chemicals Ltd., p. 61 (top); P.E.I. Premier's Office, p. 61 (middle left and bottom)